LEVEL
3

Butterflies

Laura Marsh

NATIONAL
GEOGRAPHIC

Washington, D.C.

For Aunt Jodie
— L.F.M.

Paperback ISBN: 978-1-4263-0739-3
Library binding ISBN: 978-1-4263-0740-9
UK ISBN: 978-1-4263-1804-7

Abbreviation Key: GET = Getty Images; IS = iStockphoto.com; NGS = NationalGeographicStock.com; NGT = National Geographic Television; SS = Shutterstock.com

Cover: Medford Taylor/NGS; 1, Patricio Robles Gil/Minden Pictures/NGS; 2 (centre), James P. Blair/NGS; 4 (bottom), NGT; 5 (bottom), NGT; 5 (top), John Eastcott & Yva Momatiuk/NGS; 6, Darlyne A. Murawski/NGS; 10–11 (centre), Annie Griffiths/NGS; 12, Annie Griffiths/NGS; 12–13 (top), Patricio Robles Gil/Minden Pictures/NGS; 14–15 (centre), Digital Vision/GET; 14 (centre right), M. Dykstra/SS; 15 (top right), Ambient Ideas/SS; 16–17 (centre), James L. Amos/NGS; 20 (centre), Annie Griffiths/NGS; 21 (top left), NGT; 22 (top right), Xavi Heredia/NGS; 22 (right centre), Eran Mahalu/IS; 22 (bottom right), Buck Lovell/NGS; 23 (centre), Paul Sutherland/NGS; 24 (left), Ivanastar/IS; 24 (right), Daniel Loretto/IS; 25 (left), Derek Croucher/Photographer's Choice/GET; 25 (right), Comstock/GET; 26, Artem Efimov/SS; 27 (top), Larry Minden/Minden Pictures/NGS;27 (left centre), Bianca Lavies/NGS; 28 (centre), Tom Till/Photographer's Choice/GET; 28, M. Dykstra/SS; 29 (bottom centre), NGT; 29, Ambient Ideas/SS; 30 (centre), Paul Zahl/NGS; 31 (centre), NGT; 32 (top), Paul Zahl/NGS; 32 (bottom), George Grall/NGS; 33 (bottom left), George Grall/NGS; 34–35 (centre), Cathy Keifer/SS; 36 (centre), Fotosearch; 37 (centre), Phil Schermeister/NGS; 37 (bottom right), ; 38 (top right), NGT; 38 (bottom centre), George Grall/NGS; 38 (right centre), Eric Bean/The Image Bank/GET; 38 (bottom left), NGT; 38 (bottom right), Bianca Lavies/NGS; 38 (top left), George Grall/NGS; 39 (top left), George Grall/NGS; 39 (top right), NGT; 39 (left centre), NHY59/IS; 39 (right centre), Bianca Lavies/NGS; 39 (bottom centre), James P. Blair/NGS; 40–41 (UP CTR), Mattias Klum/NGS; 41 (bottom centre), Patricio Robles Gil/NGS; 42–43, Jamie Dertz/NGS; 44 (bottom right), Donna Coleman/IS; 45 (centre), Fotosearch; 46 (top right), Biance Lavies/NGS; 46 (left centre), April Moore/NGS; 46 (right centre), Phil Schermeister/NGS; 46 (bottom left), Paul Sutherland/NGS; 46 (bottom right), NGT; 47 (top right), NGT; 47 (top right), Andy Dean/IS; 47 (left centre), Ambient Images/SS; 47 (right centre), Eric Bean/The Image Bank/GET; 47 (bottom left), Jamie Dertz/NGS; 47 (bottom right), Patricio Robles Gil/Minden Pictures/NGS; 47, Digital Vision/GET

Printed in the United States of America
14/WOR/1

Table of Contents

On the Move

When animals travel from one region or habitat to another, it is called migration. Animals migrate in search of food or a mate. Migration helps animals survive on Earth.

Many animals migrate. The monarch butterfly is one of them.

monarchs

wildebeest

red crabs

Wing Words

MIGRATION: Moving from one region or habitat to another for food or a mate

MATE: Either a male or female in a pair – most animals need a mate to have babies

Amazing Monarchs

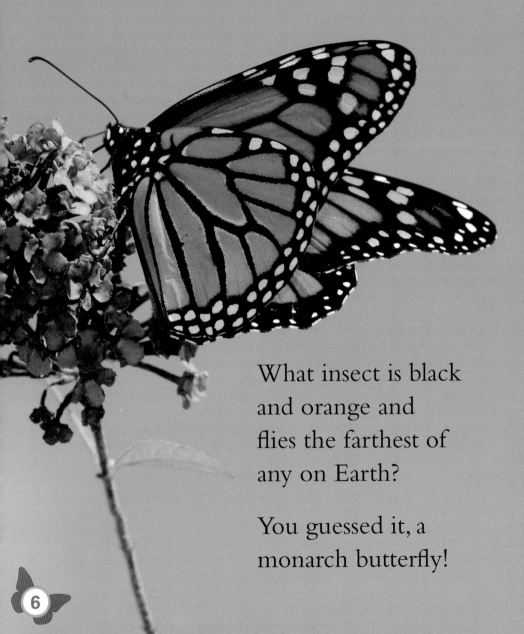

What insect is black and orange and flies the farthest of any on Earth?

You guessed it, a monarch butterfly!

Monarch butterflies migrate 3,000 to 5,000km. They travel to the forests of Mexico from the United States and Canada – and back – every year.

Since butterflies are so small, a kilometre is much farther for them than for people. A butterfly's 4,500km trip is like a person travelling over 442,000km. That's like walking around Earth 11 times!

Mighty Big Trip

Rocky Mountains

Western
Migration

Eastern
Migration

Mexico

weird
but
true

Monarch caterpillars
get oxygen through
holes in the sides
of their bodies.

Canada

United
States

Two Monarch Populations

The western population migrates along the Pacific coast of the United States. The eastern population migrates east of the Rocky Mountains in the United States and Canada all the way to Mexico. This book is about the eastern population.

It is winter.
In the Oyamel
(Oh-ya-mehl)
forests of Mexico,
clusters of butterflies
make the trees look
orange. There are
so many butterflies,
they could cover
about 11 football
fields! Here the
monarchs rest and
wait for spring.

Antennae give
butterflies a
sense of smell.

In the spring, swarms of newly awakened monarchs cover the trees and fly through the air. Millions of monarchs are ready to leave Mexico.

Need to Lead

The female monarchs lead the butterflies north from Mexico.

Their parents cannot guide them. They died soon after the eggs were laid. How do these butterflies know where to go?

The monarchs know where to go by instinct. Sunlight signals them to migrate. Scientists believe that sunlight also helps guide them.

INSTINCT: Behaviour that animals are born knowing how to do

It Takes the Whole Family

Each year, the monarchs' migration takes several generations. Three or four generations complete the trip north. But only one generation makes the return trip south.

That means that if you started the journey, your great-great-grandchildren would finish it.

How does this work?

Wing Word

GENERATION: The time it takes for a living thing to grow up and reproduce

17

The first three or four generations live two to six weeks as adult butterflies. During the spring, the first generation hatches in the south. They fly north as far as they can. Then they lay eggs and later die.

The second generation continues the journey, lays eggs and dies. The third and sometimes fourth generations hatch through the spring and summer. They finish the journey north.

weird but true

Adults appear to have four legs, but they really have six. Their two front legs are small. They are curled up and hard to see.

Canada

United States

4th

3rd

2nd

Mexico

1st

Oyamel
Forests

19

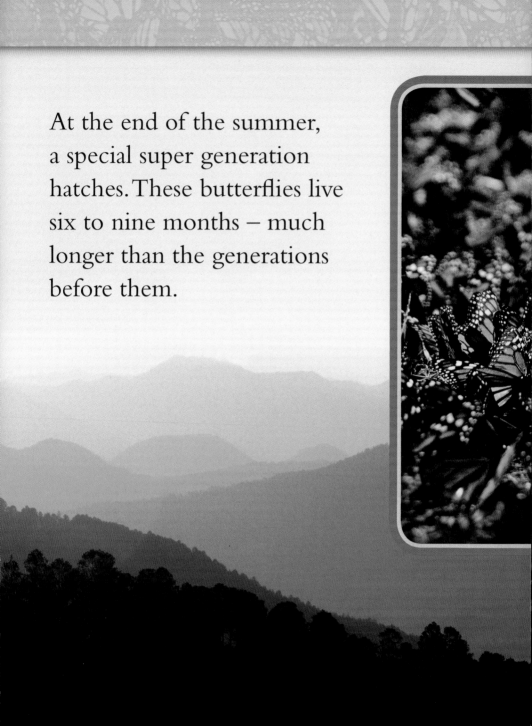

At the end of the summer, a special super generation hatches. These butterflies live six to nine months – much longer than the generations before them.

In the autumn when it gets colder in the
north, the monarchs fly south. They fly
all the way back to the Oyamel forests
in Mexico. This takes about two months.
It is a long and dangerous journey.

Danger!

Predators

Migrating butterflies make a delicious snack for many predators. To keep enemies away, monarchs have built-in protection.

Wing Words

PREDATOR: An animal that eats other animals

TOXIN: A poison from a living thing

Monarch predators include spiders, black-eared mice, praying mantises, fire ants and birds such as orioles and grosbeaks.

praying mantis

fire ants

oriole

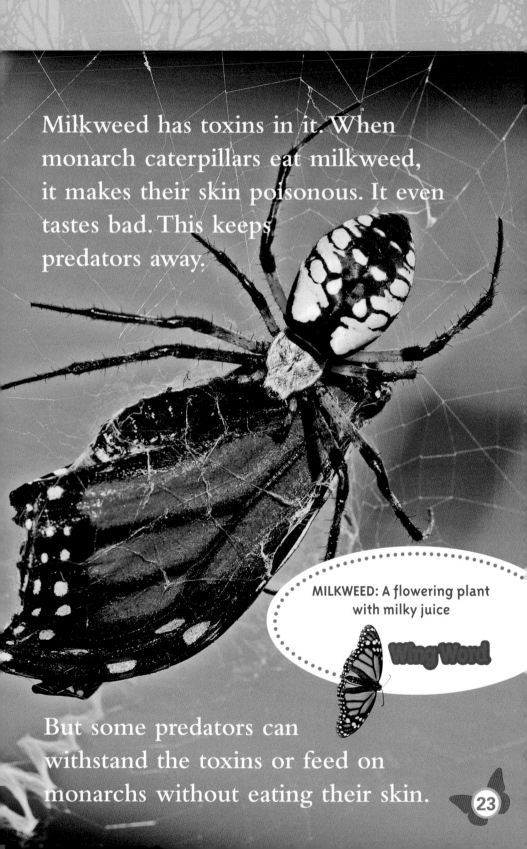

Milkweed has toxins in it. When monarch caterpillars eat milkweed, it makes their skin poisonous. It even tastes bad. This keeps predators away.

MILKWEED: A flowering plant with milky juice

Wing Word

But some predators can withstand the toxins or feed on monarchs without eating their skin.

Cold Temperatures

Monarchs need warm temperatures to fly. When temperatures get too low, monarchs will die.

Wind and Rain

Butterflies flock to the trees for shelter during high winds and rain. They cannot fly during bad weather.

How Deadly?

A rainstorm with low temperatures killed as many as 250 million monarchs in Mexico in 2002. An estimated 80 percent of the butterflies died at one of the mountain sanctuaries.

Tiring Travel

Did you know that migrating monarchs can fly up to 50km per hour? That's about three times faster than we can run.

Monarchs usually fly 80–160km a day when they are migrating. But the farthest recorded monarch travel is 430km in one day. Whew! That's tiring just to think about.

Durham   London

tag

Monarch Tracking

Scientists learn about monarchs by tracking them. Small tags are put on monarchs' wings. If a tagged butterfly is caught, the tag number, date and place are entered into a website. Then scientists know how many kilometres the butterfly flew. They also know how long it took. You can help tag monarchs, too. To find out more, go to www.monarchwatch.org.

In the winter,
monarchs rest from
their long journey.
They wake in the
spring, lay their eggs
and die soon after.

When the eggs hatch, a new
first generation begins again.
This generation will start
the journey north.

From Egg to Butterfly

There are four stages in a butterfly's life.

① Egg

A mother butterfly places her eggs on a milkweed leaf. A tiny butterfly egg is the size of a pinhead. This stage lasts four days.

Hard-Working Mamas!

A female carries up to 400 eggs. She flies from leaf to leaf. On each leaf she places only one or two eggs. That's a lot of work!

weird but true

A monarch caterpillar eats its eggshell before it starts eating milkweed.

② Caterpillar

A tiny caterpillar hatches from the egg.
It eats milkweed all day long. In two weeks
it grows from less than half a centimetre to
five centimetres long.

3 Chrysalis

A caterpillar creates a hard, protective coating around itself called a chrysalis. From outside, it appears that nothing is happening. But inside, the caterpillar is transforming into a butterfly. This stage lasts about ten days.

Wing Word

CHRYSALIS: An insect between larva and adult stage in a hardened case or cocoon

33

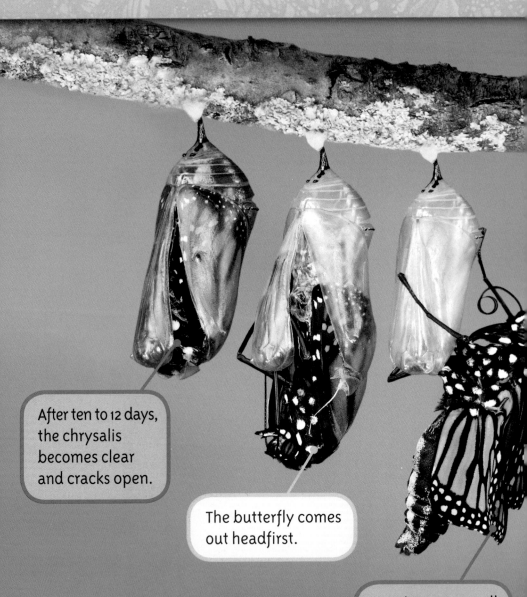

After ten to 12 days, the chrysalis becomes clear and cracks open.

The butterfly comes out headfirst.

Its wings are small and crumpled.

④ Butterfly

When the chrysalis opens, a butterfly is born!

Q Why did John throw the butter out the window?

A He wanted to see the butter fly!

The monarch pumps liquid through the veins in its wings to enlarge them.

The butterfly's veins stiffen. About one hour after it comes out of the chrysalis, the monarch is ready to fly.

Munching
Monarchs

When monarchs
are in the caterpillar
stage, they eat only
milkweed plants. And
they eat a lot!

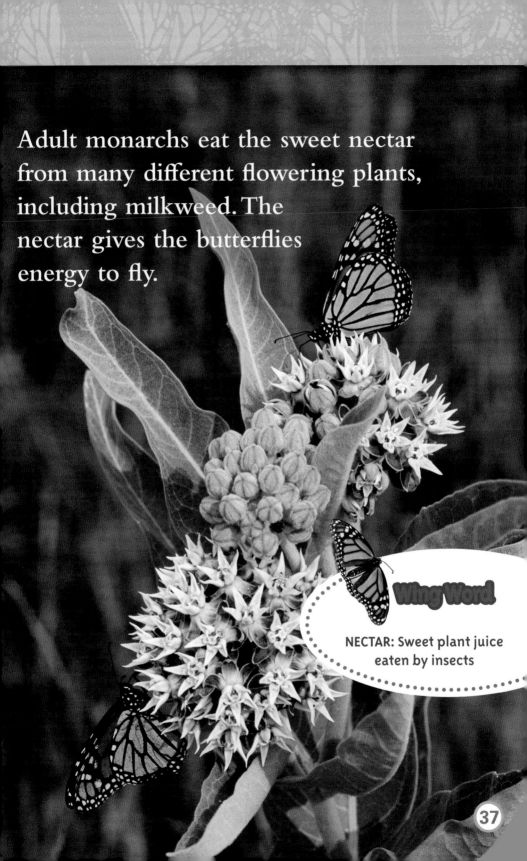

Adult monarchs eat the sweet nectar from many different flowering plants, including milkweed. The nectar gives the butterflies energy to fly.

Wing Word!

NECTAR: Sweet plant juice eaten by insects

10 Cool Things About Monarchs

1

They can flap their wings up to 2,000 times a minute.

2

Their green chrysalis looks as if it's beaded with gold.

3

An adult sucks nectar and water through its straw-like tongue, called a proboscis.

4

Their bright colours warn predators they are poisonous.

5

When caterpillars become too large for their skin, they shed it and grow new skin.

6

Predators kill 15 percent of the monarchs in Mexico every year.

7

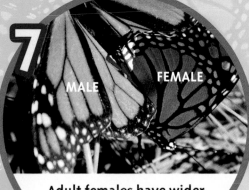

MALE FEMALE

Adult females have wider veins on their wings than males.

8

Although strong enough to fly 3,200km, a butterfly weighs less than a paper clip.

9

A newly hatched butterfly has to wait for its wings to stiffen before it can fly away.

10

Scientists think monarchs have been migrating for thousands of years.

At Risk

Humans love monarchs, but they can harm them by accident.

WingWord

HABITAT: The place or environment where a plant or animal naturally lives

In the forests of Mexico, many trees where they live have been cut down. This is called deforestation. Monarchs need trees for protection against wind and rain. Deforestation is a big problem for monarch butterflies.

WingWord

DEFORESTATION: Cutting down forests of trees

Monarchs are also losing their milkweed. People use chemicals to stop it from growing. They see milkweed as a harmful weed.

Monarch butterflies can't live without milkweed or the forests of Mexico. Humans and monarchs need to learn to share the Earth.

weird but true

Caterpillars have six pairs of tiny eyes, but they don't see well.

What You Can Do

Monarchs rarely migrate to the British Isles, but you can see lots of other beautiful kinds of butterflies here, and everyone can help them to survive and thrive.

Why not ask if you can plant a butterfly garden at home or at school? This will give butterflies a place to rest, feed and lay eggs. Fill it with their favourite plants, like lavender, and they'll soon come fluttering by!

For more ways you can help our butterflies, go to www.butterfly-conservation.org.

To find out more about monarch butterflies, check out these groups that help them:

National Geographic
http://animals.nationalgeographic.com/animals/bugs/monarch-butterfly.html

World Wildlife Fund
http://www.worldwildlife.org/species/finder/monarchbutter-flies/monarchbutterflies.html

Journey North
http://www.learner.org/jnorth/monarch/index.html

Glossary

MIGRATION: Moving from one region or habitat to another for food or a mate

GENERATION: The time it takes for a living thing to grow up and reproduce

PREDATOR: An animal that eats other animals

CHRYSALIS: An insect between larva and adult stage in a hardened case or cocoon

NECTAR: Sweet plant juice eaten by insects

MATE: Either a male or female in a pair — most animals need a mate to have babies

INSTINCT: Behaviour that animals are born knowing how to do

TOXIN: A poison from a living thing

MILKWEED: A flowering plant with milky juice

HABITAT: The place or environment where a plant or animal naturally lives

DEFORESTATION: Cutting down forests of trees

Index